An alphabet book
presented to

______________________

with love,
from

______________________

# A

illustrations
by

John Kastner

# C

Dedicated

to

all teachers

for showing us our ABCs
by text and by example

and to

Nigel and Mattie

may you and every kid out there
find the fun in learning
the alphabet with Yum and Yuk

ISBN 978-0-9844378-4-9
Library of Congress Control Number 2012907388

Achievement

is reaching your goal

by doing your personal best.

Bravery

is doing something because

it is right, even when you are afraid.

## Caring

is when you think and act

on what is correct.

CURLY
JIX

# Discipline

is doing your duties,

even when you don't feel like it.

Education

is learning about

the world we live in.

Kk Ll Mm
A + B/3 = C

Family, Friends, Fitness

make life full of fun.

# Grateful

is being thankful

for good deeds.

# Humor

is seeing

the funny side of things.

# Integrity

is about being honest

and truthful,

even when it is hard to be.

Joy

is feeling

jolly and jubilant.

JAM
JACK

# Kindness

is lending a hand

to help make others

feel better.

Love

is what you feel

when you care

about someone special.

Manners

are behaving in a way

that makes those around you

more comfortable.

M

# Neat

is when things are orderly

and in their place.

NBZ
FUN STAX
FUN STAX

# Optimism

is when you believe

everything will turn out all right

in spite of obstacles.

P

# Patience

is when you

keep the peace

by waiting your turn.

# Quiet

is when it is still enough

to hear your own breathing

so you can think and

dream uniquely,

or just simply rest.

# Respect

is recognizing that

others are different from you,

and you treat them the way

you would want to be treated.

RAT

# Sharing

is allowing others to
enjoy what you have.

# Teamwork

is working together

with others

and trusting them

to do their part.

# Useful

is doing something helpful.

UNDER DOGS
UNDER DOGS
13

Vitality

is the energy you have

with proper care

of mind and body.

# Wisdom

is when you use what you've learned

to think about what might happen

so you can make the best choice

before you say or do it.

WILLOW'S RESTA
WALDO

## eXcellence

is doing something

in the best way possible

so you can be

a good example to others.

EXIT

# Youthful

is saying "Yes" to living

regardless of

the years in your life.

# Zest

is the pizzaz

you can put into what you do

to make it more fun or snazzy!

# Z

"Act as if what you do makes a difference.
It does."

- William James, American Philosopher

**For every book sold, another will be given to a child who could use a little hand in life.**

**One for one, a Yum choice.**

The original paintings for this book were executed in gouache.

For All Ages

www.whatsupwithyuk.com

Printed in
Rochester, NY
USA